VISITOR LOG E

MW01356590

Business Name:	
Address:	
Email:	
Phone:	

NOTES

DATE	NAME	PHONE/ EMAIL	REASON FOR VISIT	TIME IN	TIME OUT	SIGNATURE

DATE	NAME	PHONE/ EMAIL	REASON FOR VISIT	TIME IN	TIME OUT	SIGNATURE

DATE	NAME	PHONE/ EMAIL	REASON FOR VISIT	TIME IN	TIME OUT	SIGNATURE

DATE	NAME	PHONE/ EMAIL	REASON FOR VISIT	TIME IN	TIME OUT	SIGNATURE

DATE	NAME	PHONE/ EMAIL	REASON FOR VISIT	TIME IN	TIME OUT	SIGNATURE

DATE	NAME	PHONE/ EMAIL	REASON FOR VISIT	TIME IN	TIME OUT	SIGNATURE

DATE	NAME	PHONE/ EMAIL	REASON FOR VISIT	TIME IN	TIME OUT	SIGNATURE

DATE	NAME	PHONE/ EMAIL	REASON FOR VISIT	TIME IN	TIME OUT	SIGNATURE

DATE	NAME	PHONE/ EMAIL	REASON FOR VISIT	TIME IN	TIME OUT	SIGNATURE

DATE	NAME	PHONE/ EMAIL	REASON FOR VISIT	TIME IN	TIME OUT	SIGNATURE

DATE	NAME	PHONE/ EMAIL	REASON FOR VISIT	TIME IN	TIME OUT	SIGNATURE

DATE	NAME	PHONE/ EMAIL	REASON FOR VISIT	TIME IN	TIME OUT	SIGNATURE

DATE	NAME	PHONE/ EMAIL	REASON FOR VISIT	TIME IN	TIME OUT	SIGNATURE

DATE	NAME	PHONE/ EMAIL	REASON FOR VISIT	TIME IN	TIME OUT	SIGNATURE

DATE	NAME	PHONE/ EMAIL	REASON FOR VISIT	TIME IN	TIME OUT	SIGNATURE

DATE	NAME	PHONE/ EMAIL	REASON FOR VISIT	TIME IN	TIME OUT	SIGNATURE

DATE	NAME	PHONE/ EMAIL	REASON FOR VISIT	TIME IN	TIME OUT	SIGNATURE

DATE	NAME	PHONE/ EMAIL	REASON FOR VISIT	TIME IN	TIME OUT	SIGNATURE

DATE	NAME	PHONE/ EMAIL	REASON FOR VISIT	TIME IN	TIME OUT	SIGNATURE

DATE	NAME	PHONE/ EMAIL	REASON FOR VISIT	TIME IN	TIME OUT	SIGNATURE

DATE	NAME	PHONE/ EMAIL	REASON FOR VISIT	TIME IN	TIME OUT	SIGNATURE

DATE	NAME	PHONE/ EMAIL	REASON FOR VISIT	TIME IN	TIME OUT	SIGNATURE

DATE	NAME	PHONE/ EMAIL	REASON FOR VISIT	TIME IN	TIME OUT	SIGNATURE

DATE	NAME	PHONE/ EMAIL	REASON FOR VISIT	TIME IN	TIME OUT	SIGNATURE

DATE	NAME	PHONE/ EMAIL	REASON FOR VISIT	TIME IN	TIME OUT	SIGNATURE

DATE	NAME	PHONE/ EMAIL	REASON FOR VISIT	TIME IN	TIME OUT	SIGNATURE

DATE	NAME	PHONE/ EMAIL	REASON FOR VISIT	TIME IN	TIME OUT	SIGNATURE

DATE	NAME	PHONE/ EMAIL	REASON FOR VISIT	TIME IN	TIME OUT	SIGNATURE

DATE	NAME	PHONE/ EMAIL	REASON FOR VISIT	TIME IN	TIME OUT	SIGNATURE

DATE	NAME	PHONE/ EMAIL	REASON FOR VISIT	TIME IN	TIME OUT	SIGNATURE

DATE	NAME	PHONE/ EMAIL	REASON FOR VISIT	TIME IN	TIME OUT	SIGNATURE

DATE	NAME	PHONE/ EMAIL	REASON FOR VISIT	TIME IN	TIME OUT	SIGNATURE

DATE	NAME	PHONE/ EMAIL	REASON FOR VISIT	TIME IN	TIME OUT	SIGNATURE

DATE	NAME	PHONE/ EMAIL	REASON FOR VISIT	TIME IN	TIME OUT	SIGNATURE

DATE	NAME	PHONE/ EMAIL	REASON FOR VISIT	TIME IN	TIME OUT	SIGNATURE

DATE	NAME	PHONE/ EMAIL	REASON FOR VISIT	TIME IN	TIME OUT	SIGNATURE

DATE	NAME	PHONE/ EMAIL	REASON FOR VISIT	TIME IN	TIME OUT	SIGNATURE

DATE	NAME	PHONE/ EMAIL	REASON FOR VISIT	TIME IN	TIME OUT	SIGNATURE

DATE	NAME	PHONE/ EMAIL	REASON FOR VISIT	TIME IN	TIME OUT	SIGNATURE

DATE	NAME	PHONE/ EMAIL	REASON FOR VISIT	TIME IN	TIME OUT	SIGNATURE

DATE	NAME	PHONE/ EMAIL	REASON FOR VISIT	TIME IN	TIME OUT	SIGNATURE

DATE	NAME	PHONE/ EMAIL	REASON FOR VISIT	TIME IN	TIME OUT	SIGNATURE

DATE	NAME	PHONE/ EMAIL	REASON FOR VISIT	TIME IN	TIME OUT	SIGNATURE

DATE	NAME	PHONE/ EMAIL	REASON FOR VISIT	TIME IN	TIME OUT	SIGNATURE

DATE	NAME	PHONE/ EMAIL	REASON FOR VISIT	TIME IN	TIME OUT	SIGNATURE

DATE	NAME	PHONE/ EMAIL	REASON FOR VISIT	TIME IN	TIME OUT	SIGNATURE

DATE	NAME	PHONE/ EMAIL	REASON FOR VISIT	TIME IN	TIME OUT	SIGNATURE

DATE	NAME	PHONE/ EMAIL	REASON FOR VISIT	TIME IN	TIME OUT	SIGNATURE

DATE	NAME	PHONE/ EMAIL	REASON FOR VISIT	TIME IN	TIME OUT	SIGNATURE

DATE	NAME	PHONE/ EMAIL	REASON FOR VISIT	TIME IN	TIME OUT	SIGNATURE

DATE	NAME	PHONE/ EMAIL	REASON FOR VISIT	TIME IN	TIME OUT	SIGNATURE

DATE	NAME	PHONE/ EMAIL	REASON FOR VISIT	TIME IN	TIME OUT	SIGNATURE

DATE	NAME	PHONE/ EMAIL	REASON FOR VISIT	TIME IN	TIME OUT	SIGNATURE

DATE	NAME	PHONE/ EMAIL	REASON FOR VISIT	TIME IN	TIME OUT	SIGNATURE

DATE	NAME	PHONE/ EMAIL	REASON FOR VISIT	TIME IN	TIME OUT	SIGNATURE

DATE	NAME	PHONE/ EMAIL	REASON FOR VISIT	TIME IN	TIME OUT	SIGNATURE

DATE	NAME	PHONE/ EMAIL	REASON FOR VISIT	TIME IN	TIME OUT	SIGNATURE

DATE	NAME	PHONE/ EMAIL	REASON FOR VISIT	TIME IN	TIME OUT	SIGNATURE

DATE	NAME	PHONE/ EMAIL	REASON FOR VISIT	TIME IN	TIME OUT	SIGNATURE

DATE	NAME	PHONE/ EMAIL	REASON FOR VISIT	TIME IN	TIME OUT	SIGNATURE

DATE	NAME	PHONE/ EMAIL	REASON FOR VISIT	TIME IN	TIME OUT	SIGNATURE

DATE	NAME	PHONE/ EMAIL	REASON FOR VISIT	TIME IN	TIME OUT	SIGNATURE

DATE	NAME	PHONE/ EMAIL	REASON FOR VISIT	TIME IN	TIME OUT	SIGNATURE

DATE	NAME	PHONE/ EMAIL	REASON FOR VISIT	TIME IN	TIME OUT	SIGNATURE

DATE	NAME	PHONE/ EMAIL	REASON FOR VISIT	TIME IN	TIME OUT	SIGNATURE

DATE	NAME	PHONE/ EMAIL	REASON FOR VISIT	TIME IN	TIME OUT	SIGNATURE

DATE	NAME	PHONE/ EMAIL	REASON FOR VISIT	TIME IN	TIME OUT	SIGNATURE

DATE	NAME	PHONE/ EMAIL	REASON FOR VISIT	TIME IN	TIME OUT	SIGNATURE

DATE	NAME	PHONE/ EMAIL	REASON FOR VISIT	TIME IN	TIME OUT	SIGNATURE

DATE	NAME	PHONE/ EMAIL	REASON FOR VISIT	TIME IN	TIME OUT	SIGNATURE

DATE	NAME	PHONE/ EMAIL	REASON FOR VISIT	TIME IN	TIME OUT	SIGNATURE

DATE	NAME	PHONE/ EMAIL	REASON FOR VISIT	TIME IN	TIME OUT	SIGNATURE

DATE	NAME	PHONE/ EMAIL	REASON FOR VISIT	TIME IN	TIME OUT	SIGNATURE

DATE	NAME	PHONE/ EMAIL	REASON FOR VISIT	TIME IN	TIME OUT	SIGNATURE

DATE	NAME	PHONE/ EMAIL	REASON FOR VISIT	TIME IN	TIME OUT	SIGNATURE

DATE	NAME	PHONE/ EMAIL	REASON FOR VISIT	TIME IN	TIME OUT	SIGNATURE

DATE	NAME	PHONE/ EMAIL	REASON FOR VISIT	TIME IN	TIME OUT	SIGNATURE

DATE	NAME	PHONE/ EMAIL	REASON FOR VISIT	TIME IN	TIME OUT	SIGNATURE

DATE	NAME	PHONE/ EMAIL	REASON FOR VISIT	TIME IN	TIME OUT	SIGNATURE

DATE	NAME	PHONE/ EMAIL	REASON FOR VISIT	TIME IN	TIME OUT	SIGNATURE

DATE	NAME	PHONE/ EMAIL	REASON FOR VISIT	TIME IN	TIME OUT	SIGNATURE

DATE	NAME	PHONE/ EMAIL	REASON FOR VISIT	TIME IN	TIME OUT	SIGNATURE

DATE	NAME	PHONE/ EMAIL	REASON FOR VISIT	TIME IN	TIME OUT	SIGNATURE

DATE	NAME	PHONE/ EMAIL	REASON FOR VISIT	TIME IN	TIME OUT	SIGNATURE

DATE	NAME	PHONE/ EMAIL	REASON FOR VISIT	TIME IN	TIME OUT	SIGNATURE

DATE	NAME	PHONE/ EMAIL	REASON FOR VISIT	TIME IN	TIME OUT	SIGNATURE

DATE	NAME	PHONE/ EMAIL	REASON FOR VISIT	TIME IN	TIME OUT	SIGNATURE

DATE	NAME	PHONE/ EMAIL	REASON FOR VISIT	TIME IN	TIME OUT	SIGNATURE

DATE	NAME	PHONE/ EMAIL	REASON FOR VISIT	TIME IN	TIME OUT	SIGNATURE

DATE	NAME	PHONE/ EMAIL	REASON FOR VISIT	TIME IN	TIME OUT	SIGNATURE

DATE	NAME	PHONE/ EMAIL	REASON FOR VISIT	TIME IN	TIME OUT	SIGNATURE

DATE	NAME	PHONE/ EMAIL	REASON FOR VISIT	TIME IN	TIME OUT	SIGNATURE

DATE	NAME	PHONE/ EMAIL	REASON FOR VISIT	TIME IN	TIME OUT	SIGNATURE

DATE	NAME	PHONE/ EMAIL	REASON FOR VISIT	TIME IN	TIME OUT	SIGNATURE

DATE	NAME	PHONE/ EMAIL	REASON FOR VISIT	TIME IN	TIME OUT	SIGNATURE

DATE	NAME	PHONE/ EMAIL	REASON FOR VISIT	TIME IN	TIME OUT	SIGNATURE

DATE	NAME	PHONE/ EMAIL	REASON FOR VISIT	TIME IN	TIME OUT	SIGNATURE

DATE	NAME	PHONE/ EMAIL	REASON FOR VISIT	TIME IN	TIME OUT	SIGNATURE

DATE	NAME	PHONE/ EMAIL	REASON FOR VISIT	TIME IN	TIME OUT	SIGNATURE

DATE	NAME	PHONE/ EMAIL	REASON FOR VISIT	TIME IN	TIME OUT	SIGNATURE

DATE	NAME	PHONE/ EMAIL	REASON FOR VISIT	TIME IN	TIME OUT	SIGNATURE

DATE	NAME	PHONE/ EMAIL	REASON FOR VISIT	TIME IN	TIME OUT	SIGNATURE

DATE	NAME	PHONE/ EMAIL	REASON FOR VISIT	TIME IN	TIME OUT	SIGNATURE

DATE	NAME	PHONE/ EMAIL	REASON FOR VISIT	TIME IN	TIME OUT	SIGNATURE

DATE	NAME	PHONE/ EMAIL	REASON FOR VISIT	TIME IN	TIME OUT	SIGNATURE

DATE	NAME	PHONE/ EMAIL	REASON FOR VISIT	TIME IN	TIME OUT	SIGNATURE

DATE	NAME	PHONE/ EMAIL	REASON FOR VISIT	TIME IN	TIME OUT	SIGNATURE

DATE	NAME	PHONE/ EMAIL	REASON FOR VISIT	TIME IN	TIME OUT	SIGNATURE

We hope you enjoyed our book !

Our goal is making your
experience a great one.

There's nothing better than reading
the valuable feedback
from you, so please let us know if
you like our book at :

eightidd@gmail.com